HAMILTON

AN AMERICAN MUSICAL BY LIN-MANUEL MIRANDA

UKULELE SELECTIONS

D1531547

ISBN 978-1-4950-8820-9

HAL•LEONARD®
7777 W. BLUEMOUND RD. P.O. BOX 13819 MILWAUKEE, WI 53213

In Australia Contact:
Hal Leonard Australia Pty. Ltd.
4 Lentara Court
Cheltenham, Victoria, 3192 Australia
Email: ausadmin@halleonard.com.au

Visit Hal Leonard Online at
www.halleonard.com

Alexander Hamilton

Words and Music by Lin-Manuel Miranda

First note

Slow (♩ = 68)

BURR: N.C.(Bm)

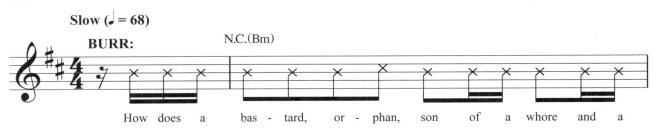

How does a bas-tard, or-phan, son of a whore and a

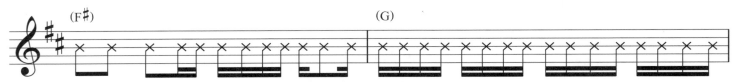

Scots-man, dropped in the mid-dle of a for-got-ten spot in the Car-ib-be-an by prov-i-dence, im-pov-er-ished, in

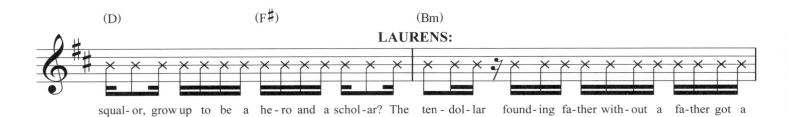

squal-or, grow up to be a he-ro and a schol-ar? The ten-dol-lar found-ing fa-ther with-out a fa-ther got a

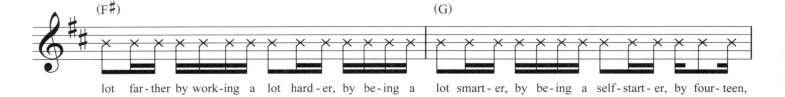

lot far-ther by work-ing a lot hard-er, by be-ing a lot smart-er, by be-ing a self-start-er, by four-teen,

JEFFERSON:

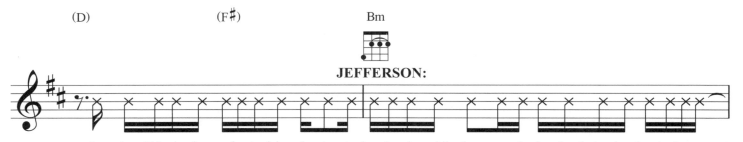

they placed him in charge of a trad-ing char-ter. And ev-'ry day while slaves were be-ing slaugh-tered and cart-ed a-way

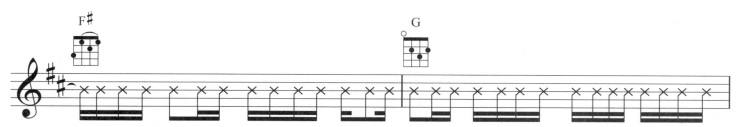

____ a-cross the waves, he strug-gled and kept his guard up. In- side, he was long-ing for some-thing to be a part of, the broth-_

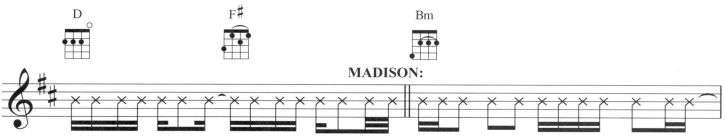

MADISON:

_er was read-y to beg, steal, _ bor-row or bar-ter. Then a hur-ri-cane came, and dev-as-ta-tion reigned, our man __

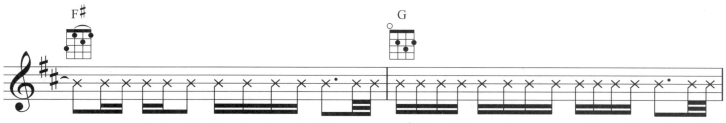

____ saw his fu-ture drip, drip-ping down the drain, put a pen-cil to his tem-ple, con-nect-ed it to his brain, and he_

BURR:

_wrote his first re-frain, a tes - ta-ment to his pain. Well, the word got a - round, _ they said, "This kid is in-sane, man."_

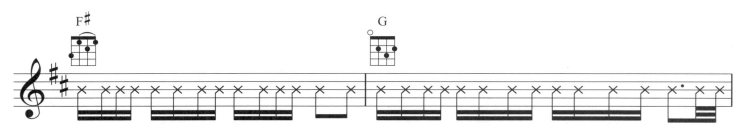

Took up a col-lec-tion just to send him to the main-land. "Get your ed - u - ca - tion, don't for-get from whence you came, and the

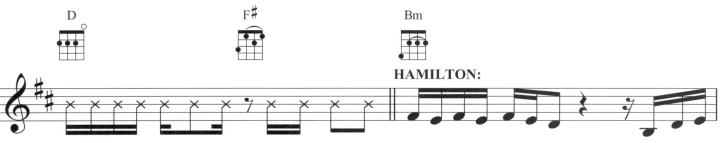

HAMILTON:

world is gon-na know your name. What's your name, man?" Al - ex - an - der Ham - il - ton. My name is

3

Al - ex - an - der Ham - il - ton. And there's a mil - lion things I have - n't done, _____ but just you

wait, _ just you _____ wait... _ **ELIZA:** When he was ten his fa - ther split, full of it, debt - rid - den two years _

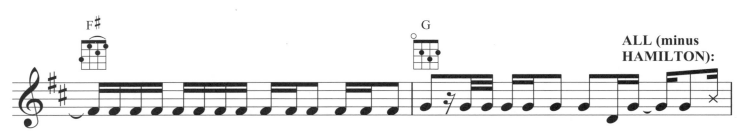

_____ lat - er, see Al - ex and his moth - er bed - rid - den, half - dead **ALL (minus HAMILTON):** sit - tin' in their own sick, the scent _ thick, and

gradual dim. to a whisper **WASHINGTON:**

Al - ex got bet - ter but his moth - er went quick. Moved in with a cous - in, the cous - in com - mit - ted su - i - cide.

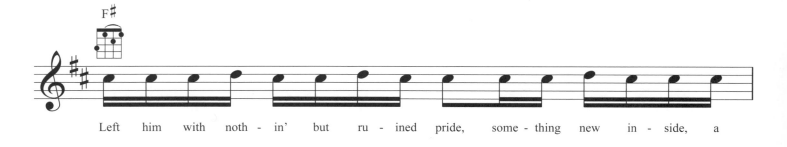

Left him with noth - in' but ru - ined pride, some - thing new in - side, a

+ ENSEMBLE: **WASHINGTON:**

voice say - in', "Al - ex, you got - ta fend for your - self." He start - ed

re - treat - in' and read - in' ev - 'ry trea - tise on the shelf. There

Bridge

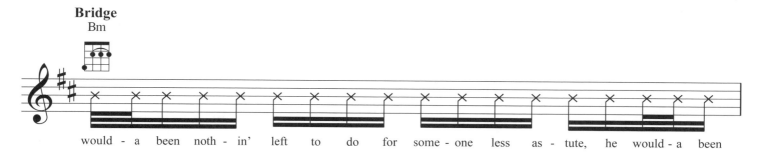

would - a been noth - in' left to do for some - one less as - tute, he would - a been

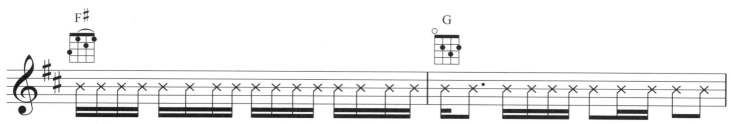

dead or des - ti - tute with - out a cent of res - ti - tu - tion, start - ed work - in', clerk - in' for his late moth - er's land - lord,

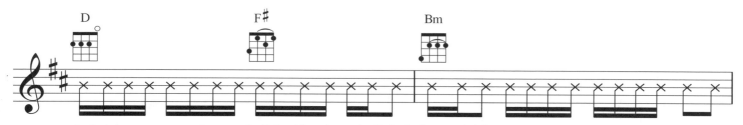

trad - in' sug - ar cane and rum and all the things he can't af - ford. Scam - min' for ev - er - y book he can get his hands on,

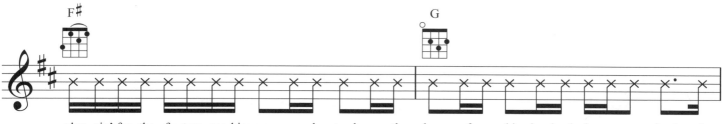

plan - nin' for the fu - ture, see him now as he stands on the bow of a ship head - ed for a new land. In

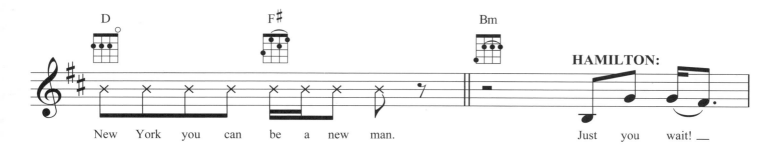

New York you can be a new man. Just you wait! __

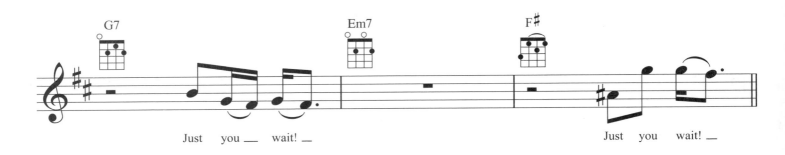

Just you ___ wait! ___   Just you wait! ___

BURR/MULLIGAN/LAURENS:

Al - ex - an - der Ham - il - ton,   Al - ex - an - der Ham - il - ton.

Wait-ing in the wings for you. ___   You nev - er learned to take your

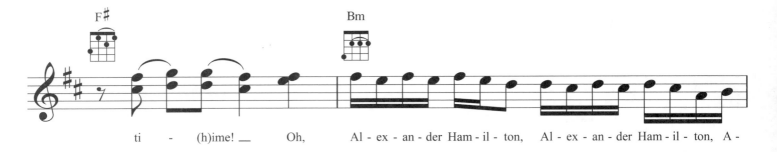

ti - (h)ime! ___ Oh,   Al - ex - an - der Ham - il - ton,   Al - ex - an - der Ham - il - ton, A -

LAURENS/MULLIGAN:

mer - i - ca sings for you. ___   Will they know what you o - ver - came? ___   Will they know ___

___ you re - wrote ___ the game? ___   The world ___ will nev - er be ___

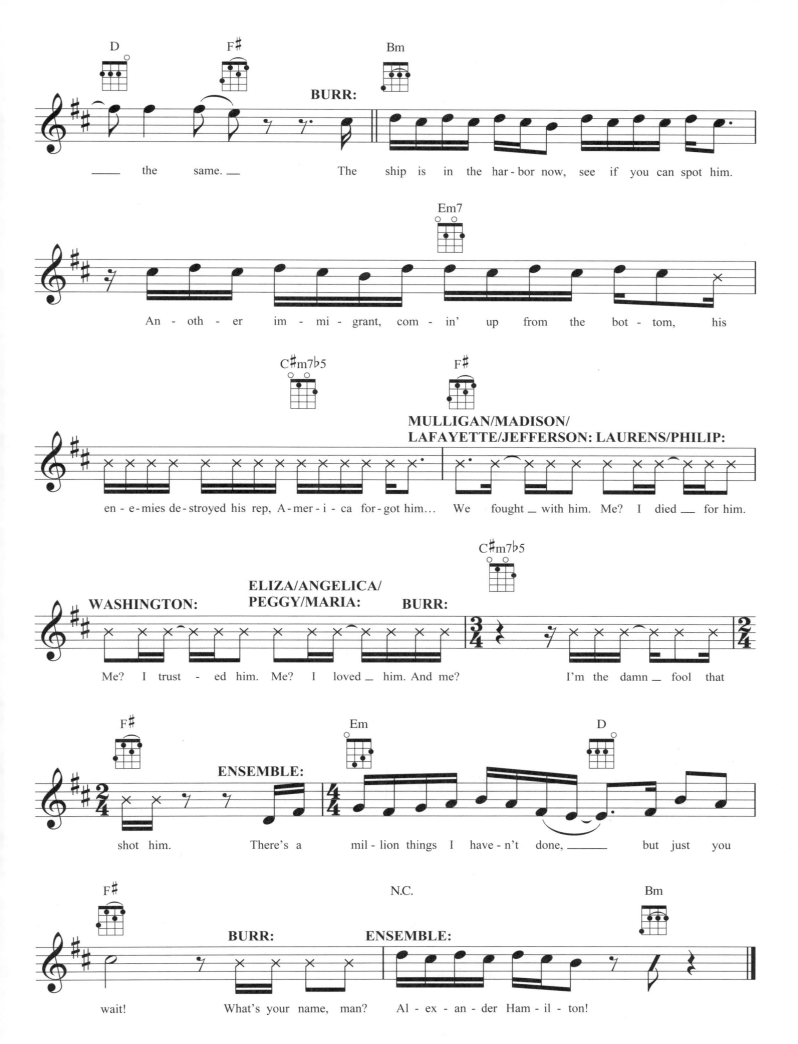

My Shot

Words and Music by Lin-Manuel Miranda
with Albert Johnson, Kejuan Waliek Muchita, Osten Harvey, Jr., Roger Troutman, Christopher Wallace

First note

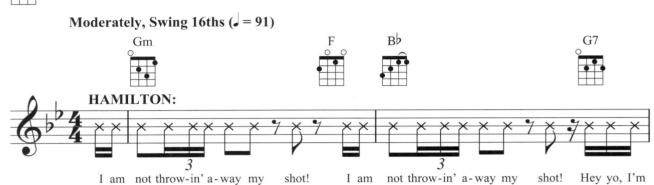

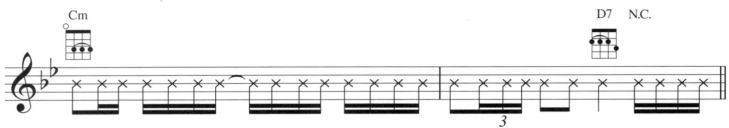

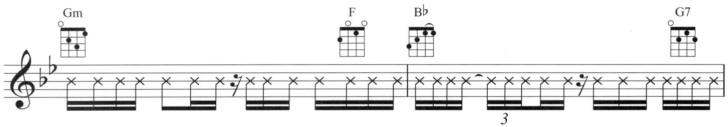

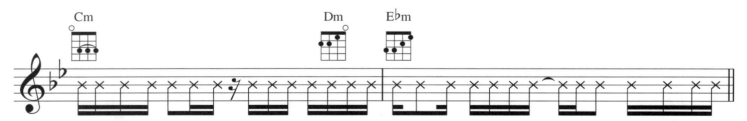

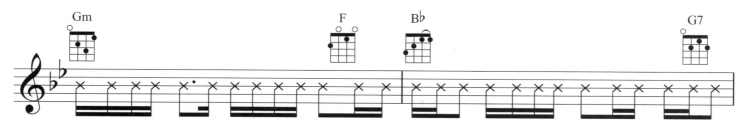

dia - mond in the rough, a shin - y piece of coal tryin' to reach my goal. My pow - er of speech: un - im - peach - a - ble.

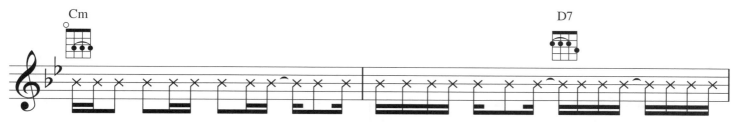

On - ly nine - teen, but my mind is old - er. These New York Cit - y streets get cold - er. I shoul - der ev - 'ry

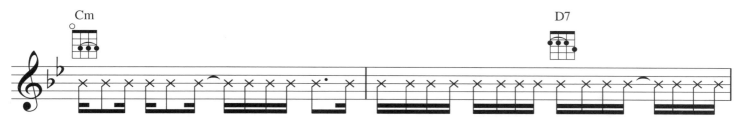

bur - den, ev'ry dis - ad - van - tage I have learned to man - age, I don't have a gun to bran - dish, I walk __ these streets fam - ished. The

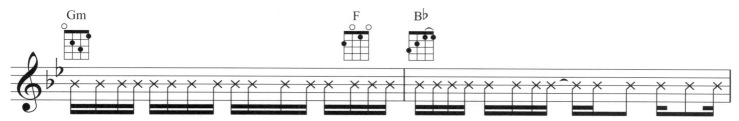

plan is to fan this spark __ in - to a flame. But damn, it's get - tin' dark, so let me spell out my name. __ I am the

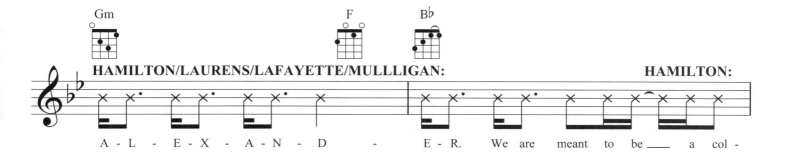

HAMILTON/LAURENS/LAFAYETTE/MULLLIGAN: **HAMILTON:**

A - L - E - X - A - N - D - E - R. We are meant to be __ a col -

o - ny that runs in - de - pen - dent - ly, __ mean - while Brit - ain keeps shit - tin' on us end - less - ly. __ Es - sen -

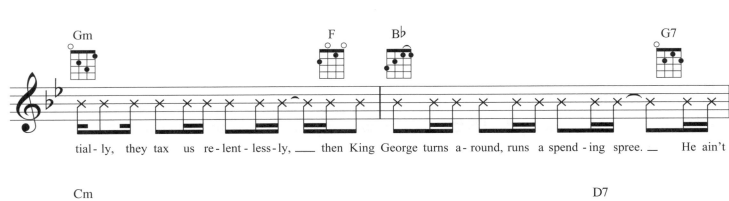

tial - ly, they tax us re - lent - less - ly, ___ then King George turns a - round, runs a spend - ing spree. ___ He ain't

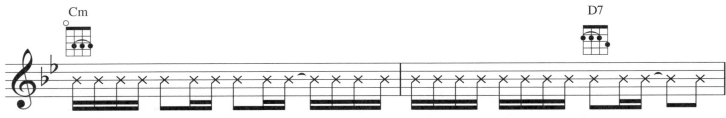

ev - er gon - na set his de - scen - dants free, ___ so there will be a rev - o - lu - tion in this cen - tu - ry. ___ En -

MULLIGAN/LAURENS/
LAFAYETTE: **HAMILTON:**

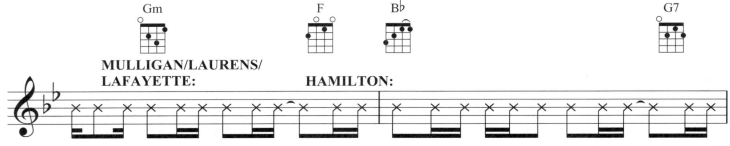

ter me! (He says in pa - ren - the - ses) ___ Don't be shocked when your his - t'ry book men - tions me. ___ I will

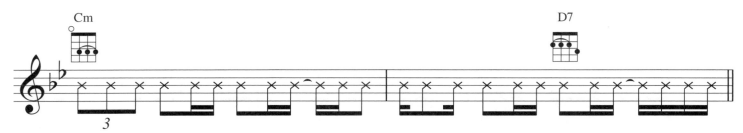

lay down my life if it sets us free. ___ E - ven - tual - ly, you'll see my as - cen - dan - cy. ___ And I am

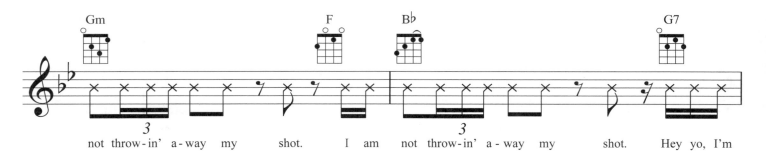

not throw - in' a - way my shot. I am not throw - in' a - way my shot. Hey yo, I'm

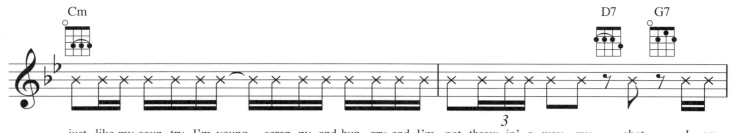

just like my coun - try, I'm young, ___ scrap - py and hun - gry, and I'm not throw - in' a - way my shot. I am

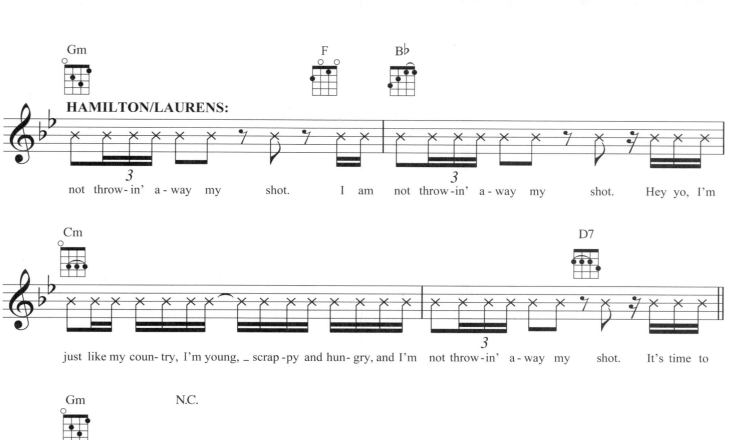

HAMILTON/LAURENS:

not throw-in' a-way my shot. I am not throw-in' a-way my shot. Hey yo, I'm

just like my coun-try, I'm young, _ scrap-py and hun-gry, and I'm not throw-in' a-way my shot. It's time to

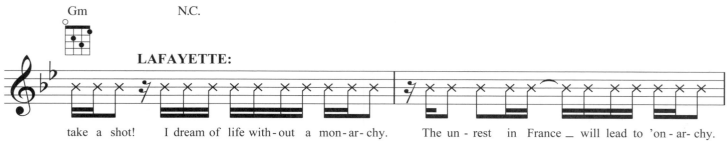

LAFAYETTE:

take a shot! I dream of life with-out a mon-ar-chy. The un-rest in France _ will lead to 'on-ar-chy.

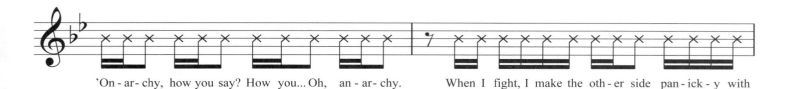

'On-ar-chy, how you say? How you...Oh, an-ar-chy. When I fight, I make the oth-er side pan-ick-y with

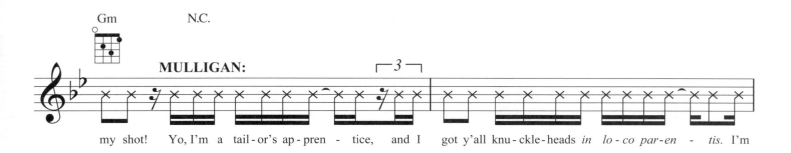

MULLIGAN:

my shot! Yo, I'm a tail-or's ap-pren - tice, and I got y'all knu-ckle-heads *in lo-co par-en - tis.* I'm

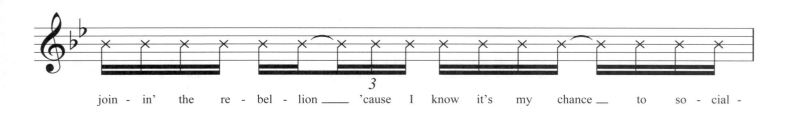

join-in' the re-bel-lion _____ 'cause I know it's my chance _ to so-cial-

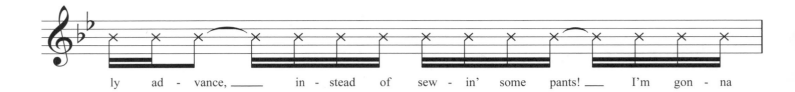

ly ad - vance, _____ in - stead of sew - in' some pants! _____ I'm gon - na

Gm   N.C.

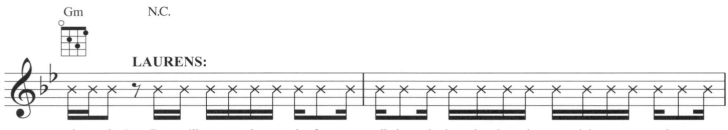

LAURENS:

take a shot! But we'll nev - er be tru - ly free un - til those in bon - dage have the same rights as you and me, you

and I, do or die. Wait till I sal - ly in on a stal - li - on with the first black bat - tal - i - on. Have an-

Gm   F   B♭   G7

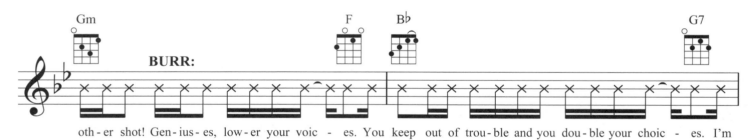

BURR:

oth - er shot! Gen - ius - es, low - er your voic - es. You keep out of trou - ble and you dou - ble your choic - es. I'm

Cm   Dm   Cm   D7

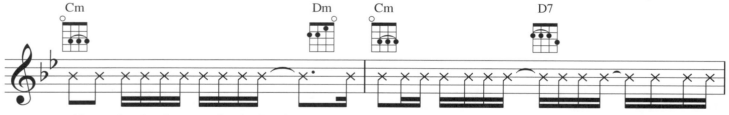

with you, but the sit - u - a - tion is fraught. _____ You've got to be care - ful - ly taught: _ If you talk, _ you're gon - na

Gm   F   B♭   G7

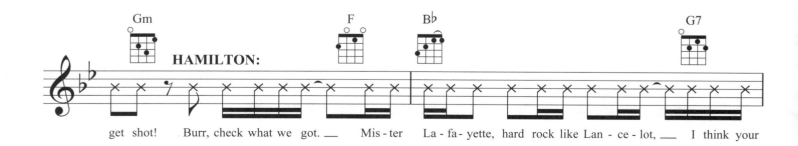

HAMILTON:

get shot! Burr, check what we got. _____ Mis - ter La - fa - yette, hard rock like Lan - ce - lot, _____ I think your

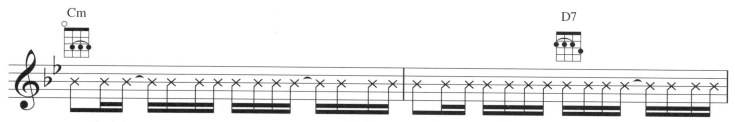

pants look hot. __ Laur-ens, I like you a lot. __ Let's hatch a plot black-er than the ket-tle call-in' the pot... __ What are the

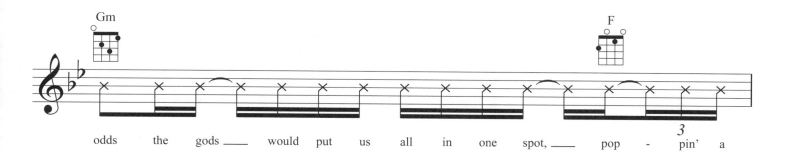

odds the gods ___ would put us all in one spot, ___ pop - pin' a

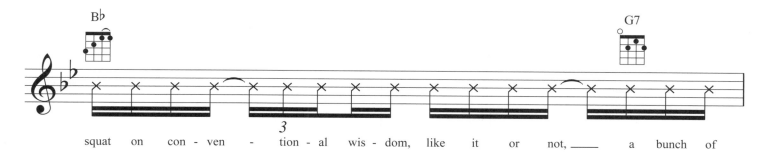

squat on con - ven - tion-al wis-dom, like it or not, ___ a bunch of

rev - o - lu-tion - ar - y man-u-mis-sion ab - o - li-tion-ists? Give me a po-si-tion, show me where the am-mu-ni-tion is!

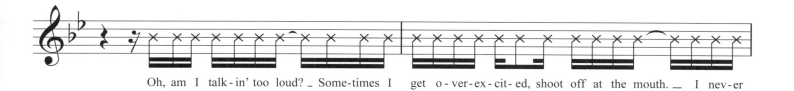

Oh, am I talk-in' too loud? __ Some-times I get o-ver-ex-cit-ed, shoot off at the mouth. __ I nev-er

had a group of friends be -fore, I prom-ise that I'll make y'all proud. __ Let's get this guy in front of a crowd. I am

not throw-in' a-way my shot. I am not throw-in' a-way my shot. Hey yo, I'm

just like my coun-try, I'm young, _ scrap-py and hun-gry, and I'm not throw-in' a-way my shot. I am

not throw-in' a-way my shot. I am not throw-in' a-way my shot. Hey yo, I'm

LAURENS:

just like my coun-try, I'm young, _ scrap-py and hun-gry, and I'm not throw-in' a-way my shot. Ev-'ry-bod-y sing:

HAMILTON/LAFAYETTE/MULLIGAN:

Whoa, _ whoa, _ whoa! _____ Hey! Whoa! _____ Wooh! Whoa! _____

LAURENS:

Ay, let 'em hear ya! Let's go! I said,

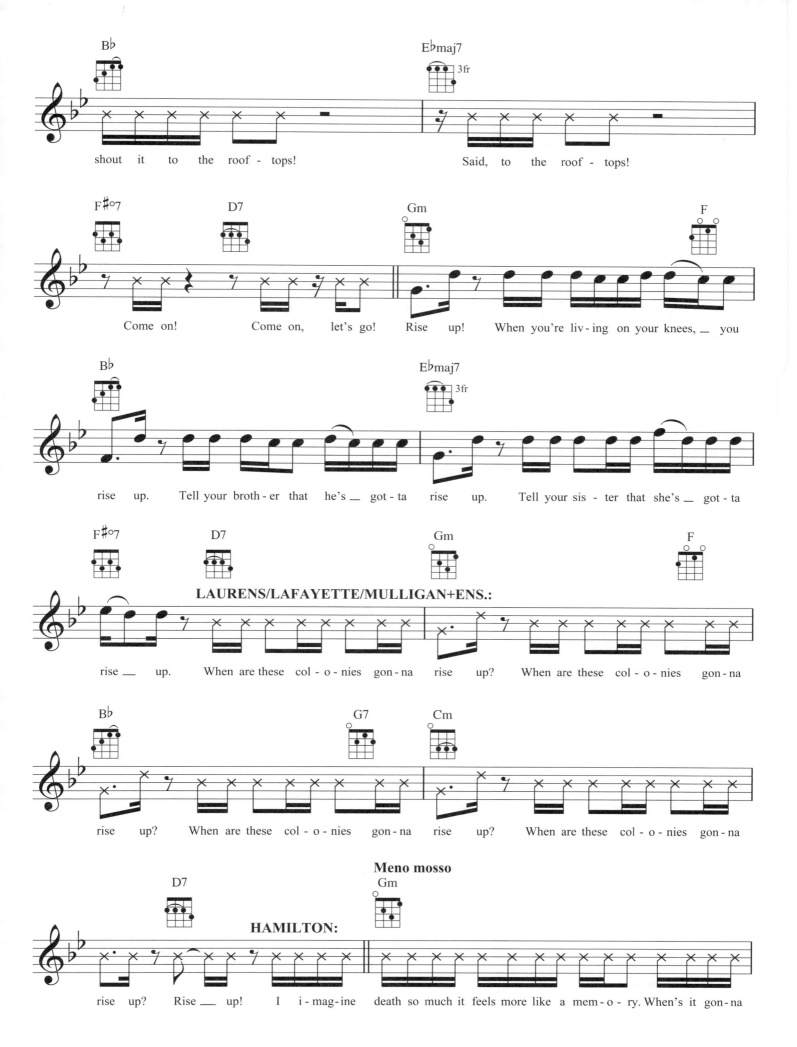

shout it to the roof - tops! Said, to the roof - tops!

Come on! Come on, let's go! Rise up! When you're liv-ing on your knees, __ you

rise up. Tell your broth-er that he's __ got-ta rise up. Tell your sis-ter that she's __ got-ta

LAURENS/LAFAYETTE/MULLIGAN+ENS.:

rise __ up. When are these col-o-nies gon-na rise up? When are these col-o-nies gon-na

rise up? When are these col-o-nies gon-na rise up? When are these col-o-nies gon-na

Meno mosso

HAMILTON:

rise up? Rise __ up! I i-mag-ine death so much it feels more like a mem-o-ry. When's it gon-na

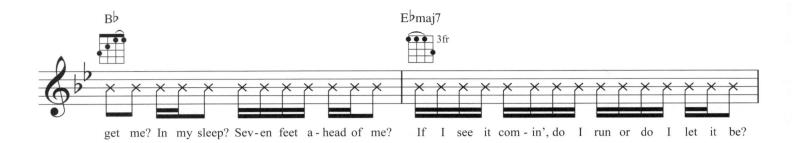

get me? In my sleep? Sev-en feet a-head of me?   If I see it com-in', do I run or do I let it be?

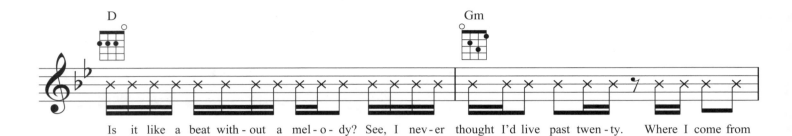

Is it like a beat with-out a mel-o-dy? See, I nev-er thought I'd live past twen-ty.   Where I come from

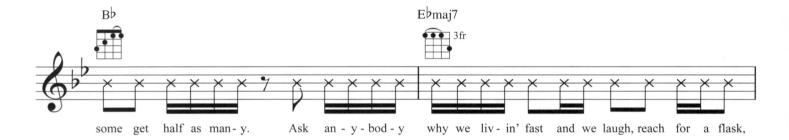

some get half as man-y.   Ask an-y-bod-y   why we liv-in' fast and we laugh, reach for a flask,

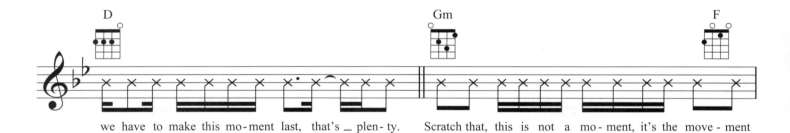

we have to make this mo-ment last, that's _ plen-ty.   Scratch that, this is not a mo-ment, it's the move-ment

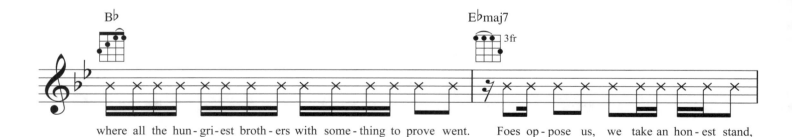

where all the hun-gri-est broth-ers with some-thing to prove went.   Foes op-pose us, we take an hon-est stand,

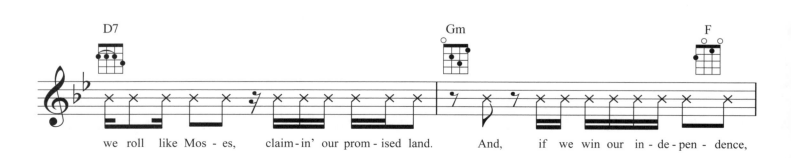

we roll like Mos-es,   claim-in' our prom-ised land.   And,   if we win our in-de-pen-dence,

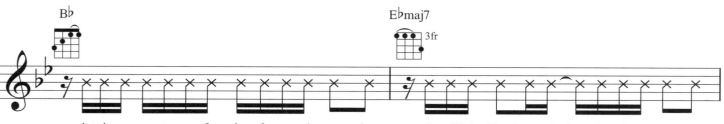

let it guar-an-tee a free-dom for our de-scen-dants. Or will the blood we shed __ be-gin an end-less

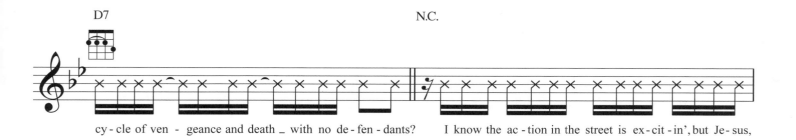

cy-cle of ven - geance and death _ with no de-fen - dants? I know the ac - tion in the street is ex-cit-in', but Je-sus,

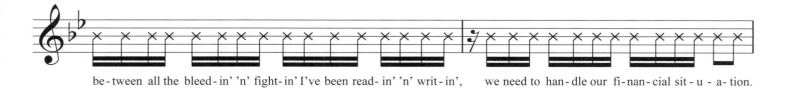

be-tween all the bleed-in' 'n' fight-in' I've been read-in' 'n' writ-in', we need to han-dle our fi-nan-cial sit-u - a-tion.

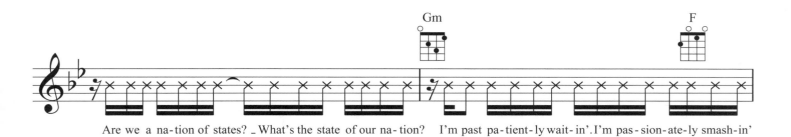

Are we a na-tion of states? _ What's the state of our na-tion? I'm past pa-tient-ly wait-in'. I'm pas-sion-ate-ly smash-in'

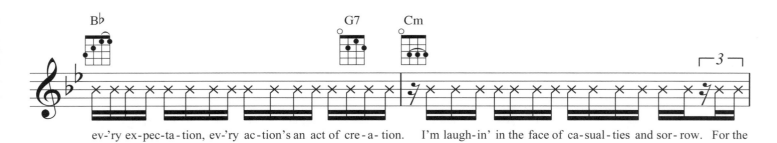

ev-'ry ex-pec-ta-tion, ev-'ry ac-tion's an act of cre-a-tion. I'm laugh-in' in the face of ca-sual-ties and sor-row. For the

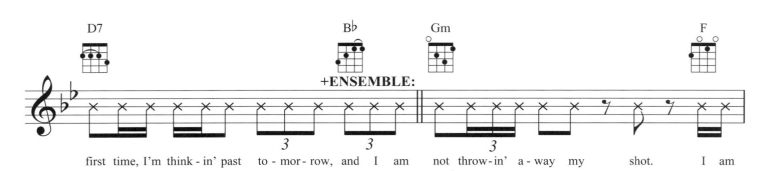

+ENSEMBLE:

first time, I'm think-in' past to-mor-row, and I am not throw-in' a-way my shot. I am

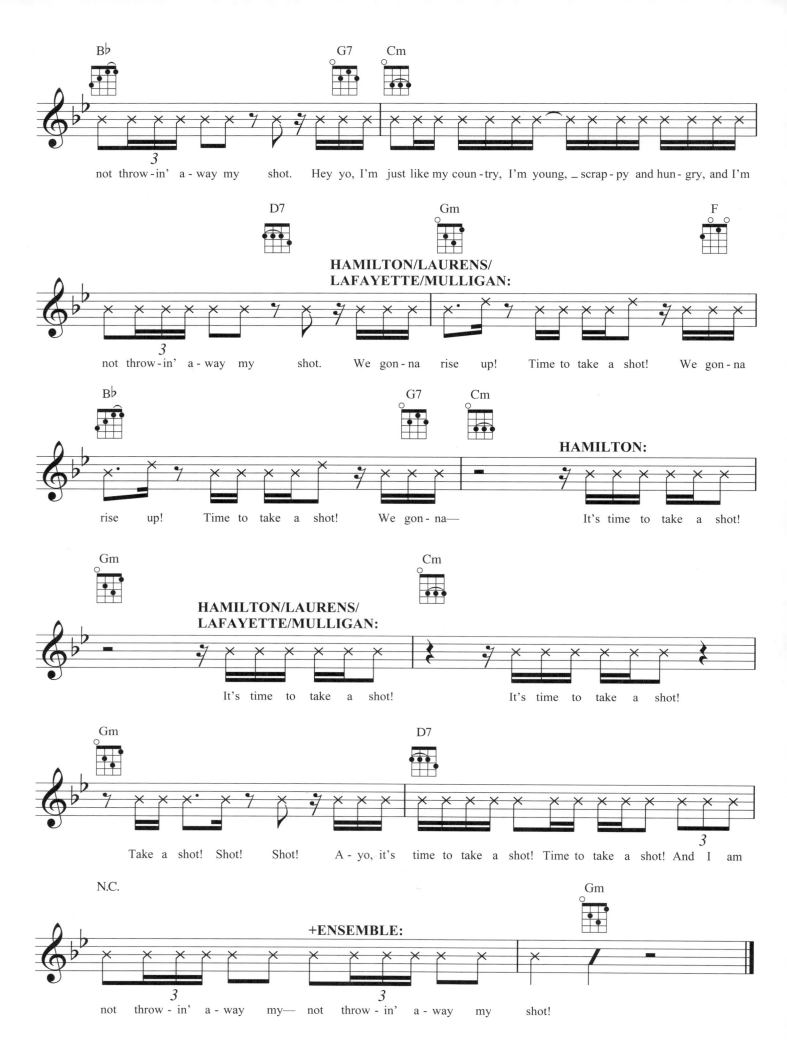

not throw-in' a-way my shot. Hey yo, I'm just like my coun-try, I'm young, _ scrap-py and hun-gry, and I'm

HAMILTON/LAURENS/
LAFAYETTE/MULLIGAN:

not throw-in' a-way my shot. We gon-na rise up! Time to take a shot! We gon-na

HAMILTON:

rise up! Time to take a shot! We gon-na— It's time to take a shot!

HAMILTON/LAURENS/
LAFAYETTE/MULLIGAN:

It's time to take a shot! It's time to take a shot!

Take a shot! Shot! Shot! A - yo, it's time to take a shot! Time to take a shot! And I am

+ENSEMBLE:

not throw-in' a-way my— not throw-in' a-way my shot!

You'll Be Back

Words and Music by Lin-Manuel Miranda

love! Da - da - da dat - da, _____ dat da - da - da da - ya - da, da - da dat

dat da - ya - da! Da - da - da dat - da, _____ dat da - da - da

da - ya - da, da - da dat dat da... _____ You say _____ our love _____ is

drain - ing and you can't go on. _____ You'll

be _____ the one _____ com - plain - ing when _____ I am gone... _____ and,

no, don't change the sub - ject 'cause you're _____ my fa - v'rite sub -

Wait for It

Words and Music by Lin-Manuel Miranda

First note

Allegro; with restrained intensity ($\quarternote = 188$)

BURR:

(echo)

The - o - do - sia writes me a let - ter ev - 'ry day (day,

day, day) I'm keep - ing her bed warm while her hus - band is a -

(echo)

way. (way, way, way) He's on the Brit - ish side in

Geor - gia. He's tryin' to keep the col - o - nies in line.

But he can keep ___ all of Geor - gia. The - o - do - sia, she's ___ mine.

Love _____ does-n't dis-crim-i-nate be-tween the sin-ners and the

saints. It takes and it takes and it takes and we _____ keep lov-ing an-y-way.

We laugh and we cry and we break and we make our mis-takes. And if _____

_____ there's a rea-son I'm _____ by her side when so _____ man-y have tried,

then I'm _____ will-ing to wait _____ for it. I'm _____ will-ing to

wait _____ for it. (wait _____ for it, wait _____ for it, wait _____ for it) My grand-fa-ther was a

(echo)

fire and brim - stone preach - er. (preach - er, preach - er, preach - er)

BURR: But there are things that the hom - i - lies and hymns won't teach ya. (teach ya,

teach ya, teach ya) **BURR:** My moth - er was a gen - ius, my

fa - ther com - mand - ed re - spect. When they died ___ they left ___

___ no in - struc - tions. Just a leg - a - cy to pro - tect. Death ___

___ does - n't dis - crim - i - nate be - tween the sin - ners and the saints. It takes and it

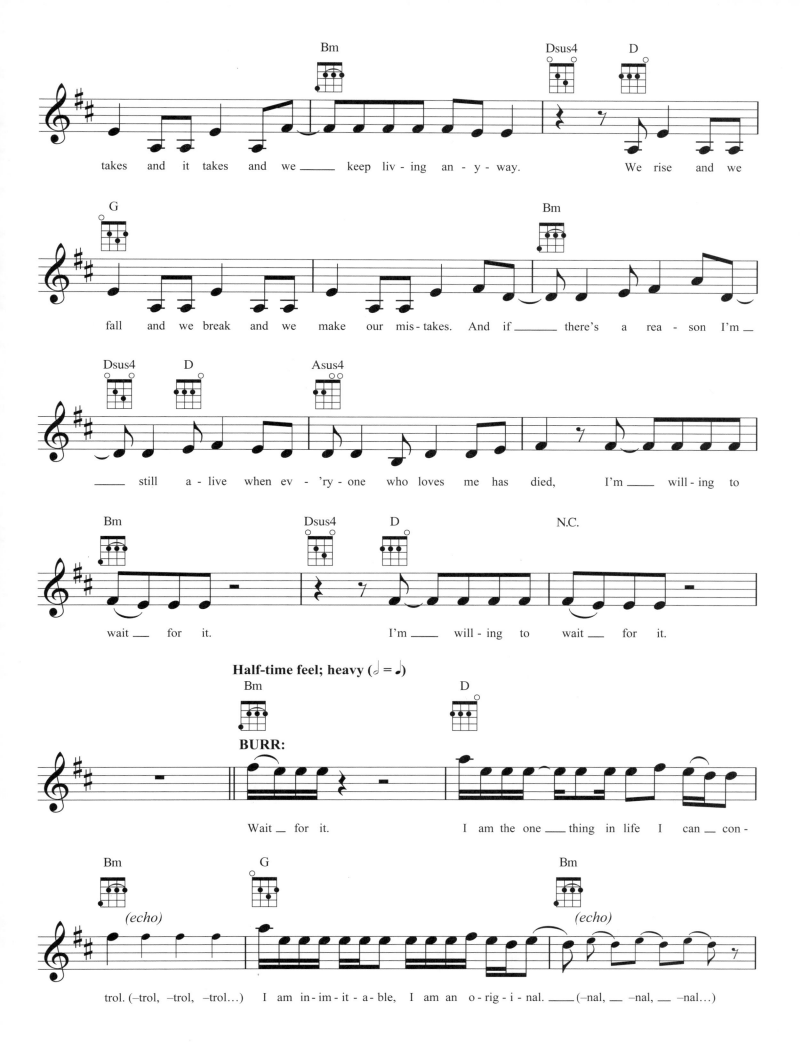

We rise _____ and we fall, _____ and if ____ there's a rea - son I'm ____ still a - live when so ____ man - y have died, ____ then I'm ____ will - ing to—

BURR: **ENSEMBLE:** Wait for it... Wait for it... Wait

BURR: **ENSEMBLE:** for it... Wait for it... Wait for it... Wait for it... Wait for it... Wait

for it... Wait for it... Wait for it... Wait for it... Wait...

That Would Be Enough

Words and Music by Lin-Manuel Miranda

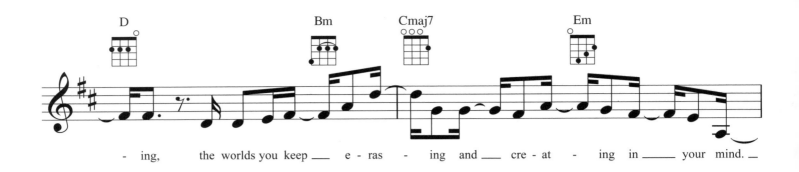

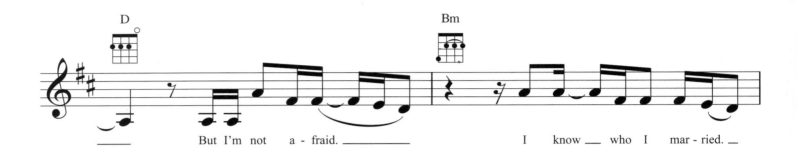

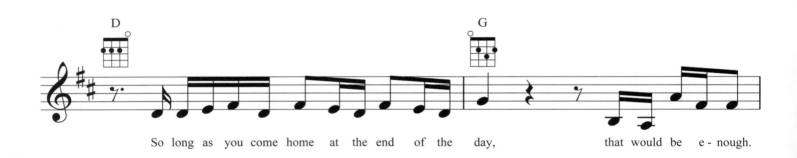

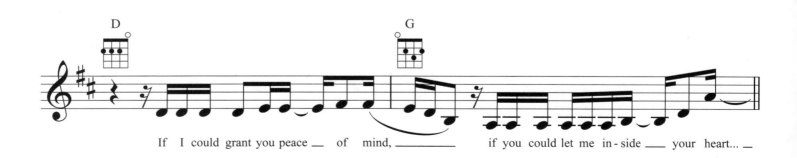

Poco più mosso

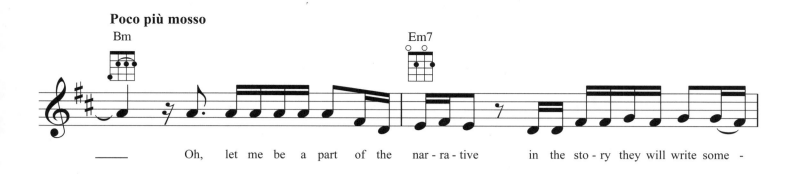

Oh, let me be a part of the nar - ra - tive in the sto - ry they will write some -

day. __ Let this mo - ment be __ the first chap - ter: __ where you de - cide to

stay, _____ and I could be e - nough,

and we could be e - nough... That would be e - nough. __

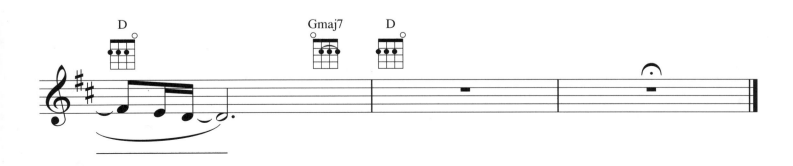

Dear Theodosia

Words and Music by Lin-Manuel Miranda

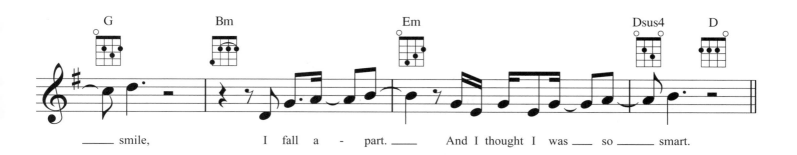

_____ smile, I fall a - part. _____ And I thought I was _____ so _____ smart.

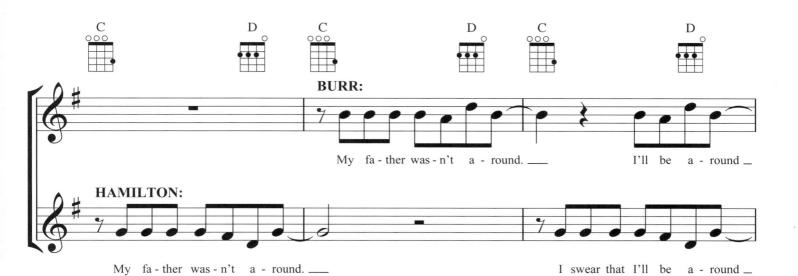

BURR:
My fa - ther was - n't a - round. _____ I'll be a - round _____

HAMILTON:
My fa - ther was - n't a - round. _____ I swear that I'll be a - round _____

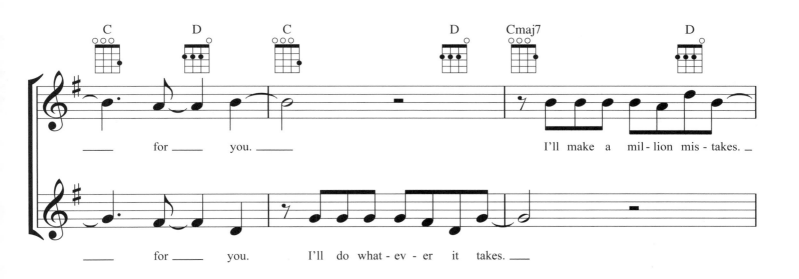

_____ for _____ you. _____ I'll make a mil - lion mis - takes. _

_____ for _____ you. I'll do what - ev - er it takes. _____

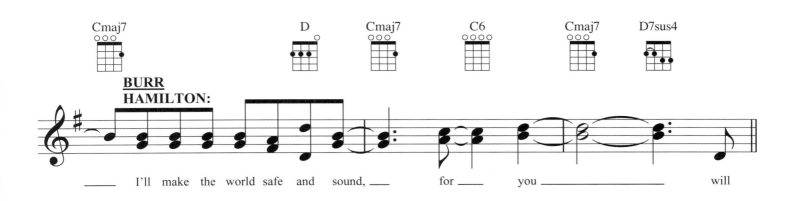

BURR
HAMILTON:
_____ I'll make the world safe and sound, _____ for _____ you _____ will

come of age with our young na - tion. We'll bleed and fight for you, ___ we'll make it

right for you. ___ If we lay a strong e - nough ___ foun - da - tion, we'll pass it

on to you, ___ we'll give the world to you, ___ and you'll blow us all a - way, ___

HAMILTON
BURR:

___ some - day, some - day. ___

Meno mosso

Yeah, you'll blow us all a - way, ___ some - day, some -

rall.

- day. ___

One Last Time

Words and Music by Lin-Manuel Miranda

First note

Moderato, Swing 16ths (♩ = 89)

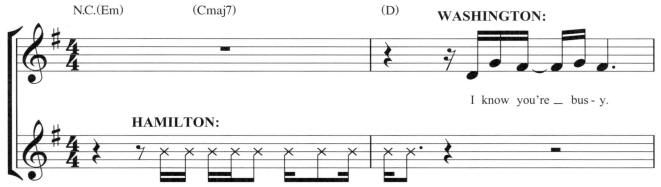

WASHINGTON:
I know you're __ bus - y.

HAMILTON:
Mis - ter Pres - i - dent, you asked to see me.

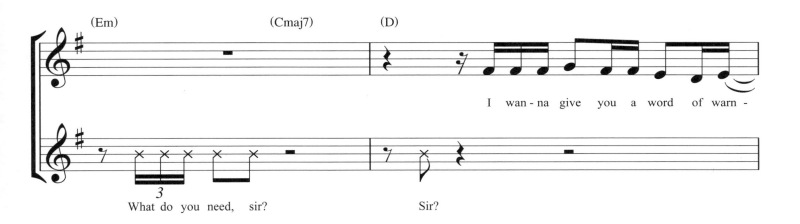

I wan - na give you a word of warn -

What do you need, sir? Sir?

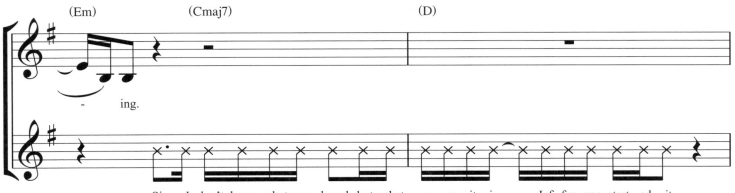

- ing.

Sir, I don't know what you heard, but what - ev - er it is, ___ Jef - fer - son start - ed it.

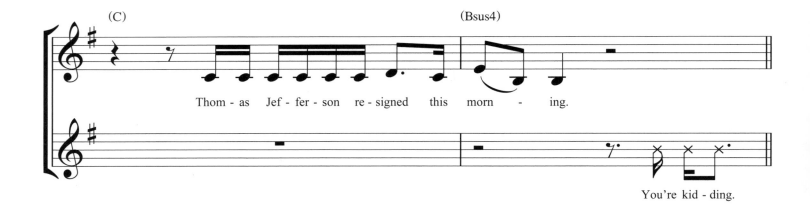

Thom-as Jef-fer-son re-signed this morn - ing.

You're kid - ding.

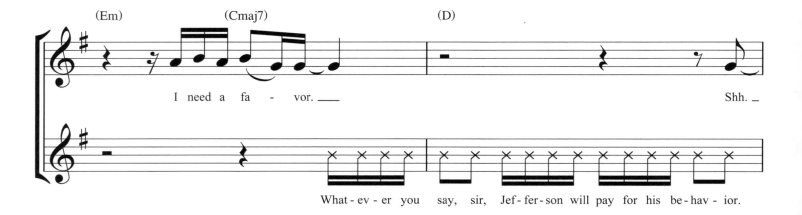

I need a fa - vor. ____

Shh. ____

What-ev-er you say, sir, Jef-fer-son will pay for his be-hav-ior.

____ Talk less!

I'll use the press, I'll write ____ un-der a pseu-do-nym, you'll see what I can do to him.

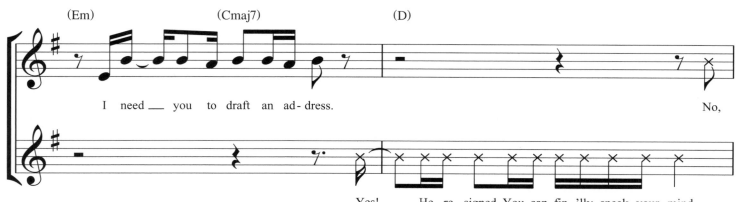

I need ____ you to draft an ad-dress.

No,

Yes! ____ He re-signed. You can fin-'lly speak your mind—

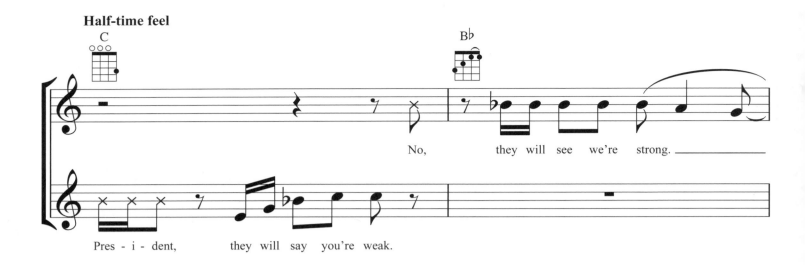

No, they will see we're strong. _____

Pres - i - dent, they will say you're weak.

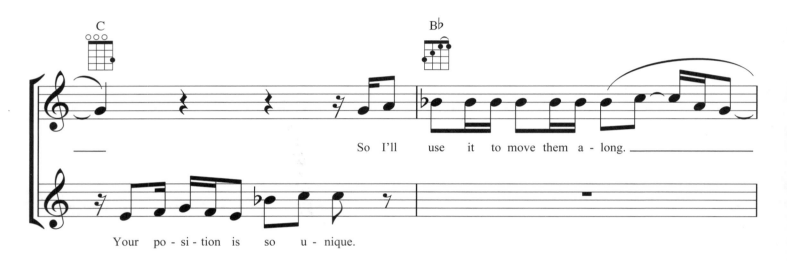

_____ So I'll use it to move them a - long. _____

Your po - si - tion is so u - nique.

_____ If I say ___ good- bye, the na - tion learns ___ to move ___

Why do you have to say ___ good - bye?

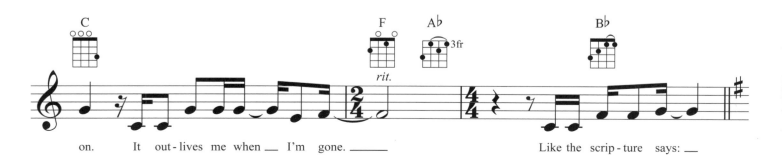

on. It out - lives me when ___ I'm gone. _____ Like the scrip - ture says: ___

Calmly, slower (♩ = 75)

N.C.

HAMILTON:

"Though, in reviewing the incidents of my administration, I am unconscious of intentional error, I am nevertheless too sensible of my defects not to think it probable that I may have committed many errors."

C   G   Am   Fm

WASHINGTON:

The hope...   view them with in - dul - gence...

HAMILTON:

keep conversational throughout

I shall al - so car - ry with me the hope   that my coun - try will view them with in - dul - gence;   and that,

C   G   F   Fm

Af - ter for - ty-five years of my life ded - i - cat - ed to its ser - vice ___ with an up - right zeal, ___

af - ter for - ty-five years of my life ded - i - cat - ed to its ser - vice ___ with an up - right zeal, ___ the

C

Con - signed ___ to o -

faults of in - com - pe - tent a - bil - i - ties ___ will be con - signed ___ to o -

46

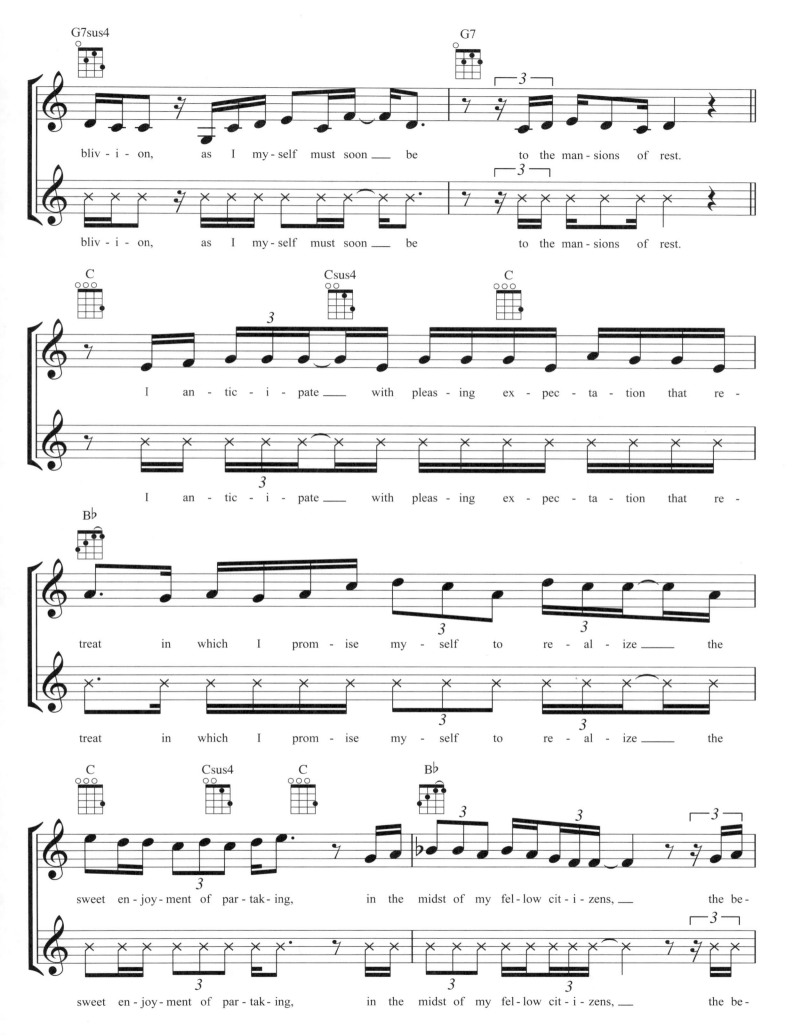

nign in-flu-ence of good __ laws un-der a free gov-ern-ment, the ev-er-fa-v'rite ob - ject of my

nign in-flu-ence of good __ laws un-der a free gov-ern-ment, the ev-er-fa-v'rite ob - ject of my

rall. poco a poco

heart, and the hap-py re-ward, __ as I _____ trust, of our mu-tu-al cares, _____

heart, and the hap-py re-ward, __ as I _____ trust, of our mu-tu-al cares, __

A tempo, Swing 16ths (♩ = 89)

la - bors, and dan - gers. One last __ time... __

la - bors, and dan - gers.

HAMILTON:
poco accel.

Teach 'em how to say ___ good-bye...

WASHINGTON: *ad lib. to end*

You and I! ____

Hurricane

Words and Music by Lin-Manuel Miranda

out. _____ I looked up and the town had its eyes ___ on ___ me. _

_____ They passed a plate a - round. _____ To - tal stran -

- gers, moved ___ to kind - ness by _____ my ___

sto - ry, raised e - nough for me to book pas - sage on a ship that was

Più mosso (♩ = 87)

poco accel.

New York - bound... I wrote my way out of hell. __ I wrote my way to rev - o -

lu - tion. I was loud - er than the crack in the bell. __ I wrote E - li - za love let - ters un - til she fell. I wrote a -

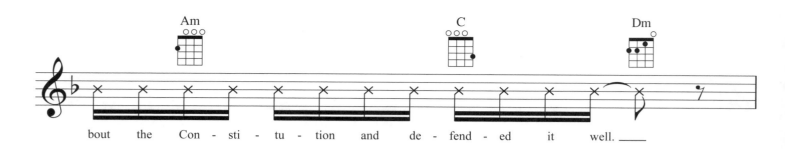

bout the Con - sti - tu - tion and de - fend - ed it well. ___

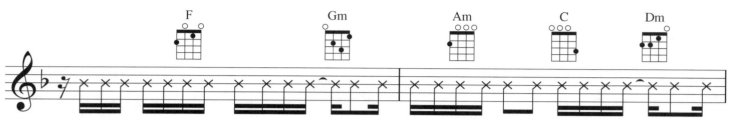

And in the face of ig - no - rance and re - sis - tance, I wrote fi - nan - cial sys - tems in - to ex - is - tence. And

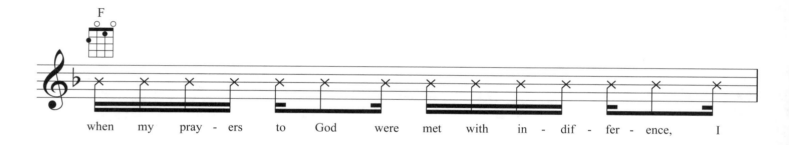

when my pray - ers to God were met with in - dif - fer - ence, I

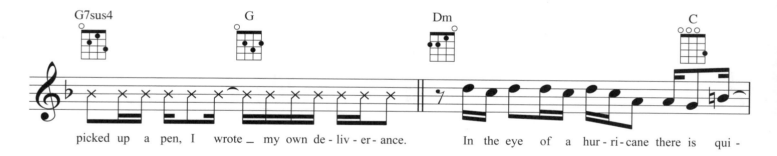

picked up a pen, I wrote ___ my own de - liv - er - ance. In the eye of a hur - ri - cane there is qui -

- et for just a mo - ment, a

yel - low sky. ___ I was twelve when my moth - er died. ___ She was

Burn

Words and Music by Lin-Manuel Miranda

First note

Moderate 2, icy (♩. = 66)

keep vocal rhythms
conversational throughout

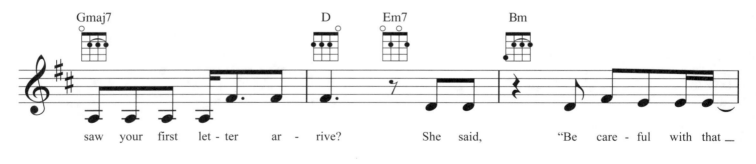

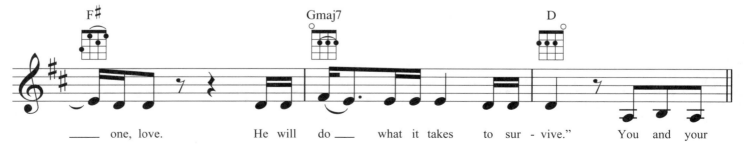

words flood - ed my sens - es. ____ Your sen - tenc - es left me de -

fense - less. You built me pal - ac - es ____ out of par - a - graphs, you built ca -

the - drals. __ I'm re - read - ing the let - ters you wrote me. ____ I'm

search - ing and scan - ning for an - swers in ev - er - y line, for some kind of

sign, and when you were ____ mine, ____ the world __ seemed ____ to burn. ____

_____ Burn. _____

world has ___ no right to my ___ heart. The world has no place in our bed. They

don't get ___ to know what I said. I'm burn-ing the mem-o-ries, burn-ing the

let-ters that might have re - deemed ___ you. ___ You for - feit all rights to my ___

heart. You for - feit ___ the place in our bed. You sleep in your of - fice in - stead, with on - ly ___ the

mem-o-ries of when you were ___ mine. ___

I hope that you   burn. ___

It's Quiet Uptown

Words and Music by Lin-Manuel Miranda

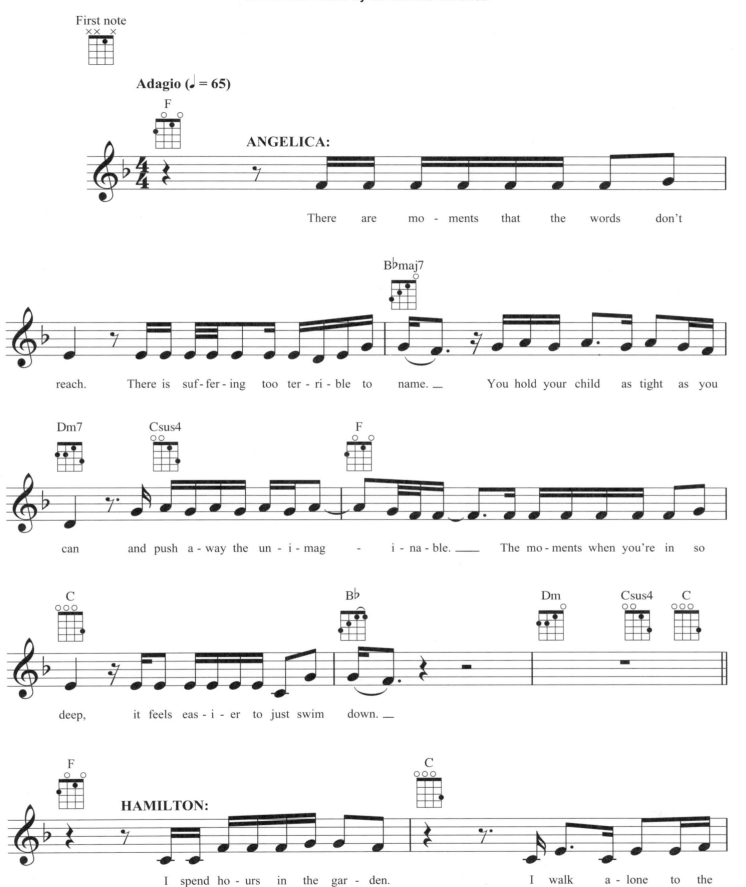

store.   And it's qui - et up - town.   I nev - er liked the qui - et be - fore. __

__   I take the chil - dren to church on Sun - day,   a sign of the cross at the door, __

__   and I _____ pray.   That nev - er used to hap - pen be - fore. __

__   Phil - ip, you would like it up - town. It's

qui - et up - town.

You knock me out, ___ I _____ fall a - part. ___

60

- ing what ___ we've lost _____ and you need time. __

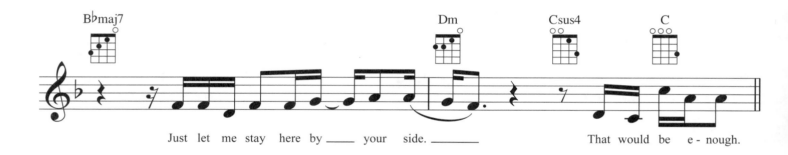

___ But I'm not a - fraid. _____ I know __ who I mar - ried.

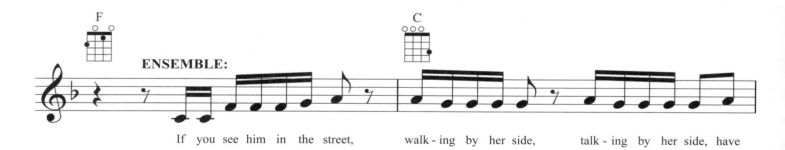

Just let me stay here by ___ your side. _____ That would be e - nough.

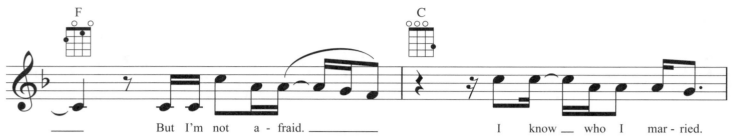

ENSEMBLE: If you see him in the street, walk - ing by her side, talk - ing by her side, have

HAMILTON: E - li - za, do you like it up - town? It's qui - et up - town.

pit - y.

He is try'ng to do the un - i - mag -

- i - na - ble. _____ See them walk - ing in the park,

long _____ af - ter dark, tak - ing in the sights of the

HAMILTON:

cit - y. Look a - round, _ look a - round, _ E - li - za! ____

ANGELICA:

There are mo - ments that the words don't reach. There's a grace too pow - er - ful to

name. _ We push a - way what we can nev - er un - der - stand, we push a - way the un - i - mag -

i - na - ble. They are stand - ing in the gar - den, Al - ex - an - der by E - li - za's